Oh, Hell!

Two One-Act Plays

Bobby Gould in Hell
by David Mamet

The Devil and Billy Markham
by Shel Silverstein

A SAMUEL FRENCH ACTING EDITION

FOUNDED 1830

New York Hollywood London Toronto

SAMUELFRENCH.COM

IMPORTANT BILLING AND CREDIT REQUIREMENTS

BOBBY GOULD IN HELL

Bobby Gould in Hell premiered at Lincoln Center in December, 1989 under the direction of Gregory Mosher, with setting by John Lee Beatty, costumes by Jane Greenwood, lighting by Kevin Rigdon, sound by Bill Dreisbach, illusionist effects by George Schindler, and with the following cast:

BOBBY GOULD .... Treat Williams
INTERROGATOR'S
    ASSISTANT .... Steven Goldstein
THE INTERROGATOR .... W. H. Macy
GLENNA .... Felicity Huffman

CHARACTERS

Bobby Gould
Interrogator's Assistant
The Interrogator
Glenna

BOBBY GOULD IN HELL

AT RISE: BOB and ASSISTANT sitting around in hell.

(Pause.)

 BOB. Have you been down here long?
 ASSISTANT. Shhh!

(THUNDER and LIGHTNING.
INTERROGATOR enters, dressed in waders and festooned
 with fishing gear.)

 INTERROGATOR. Guess where I was going this
morning?
 BOB. Fishing.
 INTERROGATOR. I was going fishing. That is true.
That is one of the subset of things in the world which are
true. I am not going fishing now. No. I am here. I do not
want to be here. I am here. But these things happen. Don't
they?
 BOB. Yes.
 INTERROGATOR. They happen.
 BOB. Yes.
 INTERROGATOR. How can we tell?
 BOB. Please?
 INTERROGATOR. How can we tell that they happen?

(Pause.)

 BOB. Because they are happening.

INTERROGATOR. Because they are happening. Is that
your answer?

BOB. Yes.

INTERROGATOR.   (*To Bob.*) You ever felt
Helpless...?

BOB. Have I ...?

INTERROGATOR. You know. Where things are
happ'ning Out of Your Control?

BOB. Yes.

INTERROGATOR. You have...

BOB. Yes, I have.

INTERROGATOR. And it felt "Bad." It felt "Bad."

BOB. Yes.

INTERROGATOR. I had planned to go "fishing." I was
called to come here. It felt bad. You could wish for an end
To Your Feelings, but, then, you wouldn't *feel* anything.
Would you...?

BOB. No.

INTERROGATOR. And *then* where would you be?

BOB. I want to go home.

INTERROGATOR. What is real?

BOB. I don't understand.

INTERROGATOR. Indeed you don't. "I'm Thinking of
a Number." What is real?

BOB. You're thinking of a number.

INTERROGATOR. What is real? Is the "number" real?
Are *you* real...?

BOB. I want to go home.

INTERROGATOR. Are "feelings" real?

BOB. ...are feelings real...

INTERROGATOR. Yes.   Are "thoughts" real? Play
along with me here...

BOB. Are thoughts real?

INTERROGATOR. Yes.

BOB. They are real...

INTERROGATOR. Yes.

BOB. In that we "think" them.

INTERROGATOR. In that we 'think' them. I see.

BOB. I'd like to go home. You know, there's been a mistake made, and I'd like to go home.

ASSISTANT. (*Writing.*) ... a mistake made ...

(*BOBBY, trying to escape, runs to large set of double doors. HE opens double doors, finds the SIGHTS and SOUNDS of Hell, flames, and screams, etc. HE closes the doors and sits back down.*)

BOB. I don't belong here.

INTERROGATOR. No?

BOB. I'm a Good Man.

INTERROGATOR. Are you...?

BOB. It may be that this or that in my life has...

INTERROGATOR. (*Pause.*) Has what? Caused pain? Been bad? What? Say you're a Bad Man, and I'll go easy on you.

BOB. Wait, wait, wait a second, you'll "Go Easy" on me?

INTERROGATOR. Yes.

BOB. What does that mean? If I say I'm a "Bad Man," you'll send me back...?

INTERROGATOR. Oh, Lordy, No. It doesn't mean *that*, no.

BOB. I'm supposed to stay down here ... for ... how long?

ASSISTANT. Imagine a stone mountain one hundred miles high and every ten thousand years a small bird comes and pecks once at the mountain with his beak and flys away and when that mountain has been pecked away to dust your stay here will have just begun.

INTERROGATOR. And will that be longer or shorter than that speech? You know "a long long time" would have done just as well. If they ask how long they're going to stay down here just say "a long long time." (*To Bob.*) Say you're a bad man.

BOB. What? No.

INTERROGATOR. Say it.

BOB. No.

INTERROGATOR. Say it.

BOB. No, I have a headache.

INTERROGATOR. A headache. You know what's good for that...asprin.

BOB. I should take an asprin.

INTERROGATOR. "Take" an asprin. No. I meant the "*existence* of asprin is good for a headache." It's what they call "non-invasive therapy." Isn't it something? What they-all can *do* nowdays? You know, they say "I miss the old days," but *I* say, for everything that we lose, we gain something *new*. Innit? Eh?

BOB. Could I have an asprin?

INTERROGATOR. *No*, you couldn't have an asprin, you dumb shit, you're put here to *suffer*. Say you're a Bad Man.

BOB. I've had a long day.

INTERROGATOR. Have you...? Well. What a funny world it is. And how Alike we are. (*HE reads from the large Book of All the Deeds of Humanity.*) Why'd *you* grow the long nails? (*HE puts the book down.*)

BOB. The long nails...

INTERROGATOR. Yes.

BOB. For sex.

INTERROGATOR. With whom?

BOB. With a woman.

INTERROGATOR. What woman? (*Pause.*)

BOB. A woman that I know.

NTERROGATOR. Uh huh—To hurt her.
BOB. No.
INTERROGATOR. To "tickle" her.
BOB. No.
INTERROGATOR. To scratch her. To titillate her.
BOB. Yes.
INTERROGATOR. And you had no desire to hurt her?
BOB. No.
INTERROGATOR. You said ... (*ASSISTANT hands him a file.*) "I want to kill you and eat you." That's diverting, now ... you didn't want to hurt her?
    BOB. I want to go home.
INTERROGATOR. (*To Bob.*) No, no, you can't go home.
    BOB. I have done nothing to warrant my being down here.
    INTERROGATOR. Oh, Dash it all to flinders, then, there's been a mistake made!
BOB. Yes.
INTERROGATOR. Let me see that book. (*Browses through the book.*)
    BOB. And, I would say, on the curve, I was a, if you will, I was a straight B-Minus sort of man.
    INTERROGATOR. Very ingenuous ... You said ... (*Of book.*) Oh. I lost it... (*To Assistant.*) Something, something that he wanted to shove up her ass ...
    ASSISTANT. He wanted to shove something up her ass.
    INTERROGATOR. It's in the rep ... didn't you read the report? Oh, fuck me. Don't bother to lie. You'd *read* it, how could you forget the ... he wanted to... (*HE checks the file.*) He wanted to shove a...
    ASSISTANT. A *Toaster!*
    INTERROGATOR. (*Pause.*) Why couldn't you say so?
    ASSISTANT. I'd forgotten it.

INTERROGATOR. I can hardly credit that.

BOB. I want to go home.

INTERROGATOR. Uh huh. You're a bad 'un, you are. "Want to go home..." *You disembowelled this young girl!* You *could* have screwed the lass, come like a gentleman, lay back, smoke your cig, passed the time joshing her about: "Two gentlemen of Hebraic extraction go into a bar..." (*To Assistant.*) take it up.

ASSISTANT. Sir?

INTERROGATOR. You heard me.

ASSISTANT. ...they go into a bar...

INTERROGATOR. ... they're *in* the bar.

ASSISTANT. and one says "I think I'll have a drink" (*Pause.*) The *other* one says... (*Long pause.*)

INTERROGATOR. Oh, God, am I quite alone ... am I the wee-est bit alone? (*Sighs.*)

BOB. Um...?

INTERROGATOR. No, don't try to comfort me.

BOB What about if the one said "How about a drink?" and the *other* one said he couldn't *have* a drink, because it was some sort of a religious holiday.

INTERROGATOR. Uh huh. What sort of a religious holiday? (*Pause.*)

BOB. One in which they didn't allow drinking.

INTERROGATOR. ... One in which they didn't allow drinking ... so it wouldn't be a *celebration*, it would be a, what, a day of *fasting*...

BOB. ...Yes.

INTERROGATOR. ... of "*mortification*"...

ASSISTANT. What about if they weren't Jews?

BOB. Oh, I remembered something.

INTERROGATOR. ...and so they wouldn't be "*able*" to have a drink...

BOB. No.

ASSISTANT. What about if they weren't Jews?

BOB. No, I don't think that's the problem.

INTERROGATOR. I don't either.

ASSISTANT. No...?

BOB. Oh, I remembered something.

INTERROGATOR. Yes. Yes, Little One. You remembered something. You remembered what?

BOB. It gave me pleasure.

INTERROGATOR. "It" gave you pleasure...

BOB. Yes. To *scratch* her.

INTERROGATOR. Good. *(Pause.)* What *is* "pleasure?" No, just kidding. Good. Well. Now we're on to something...! You scratched her, she liked it. You felt it made you some, it made you something more of a "man..." to "Please" her ... something of that sort. And I can understand that, being a man myself. Is that the thing?

BOB. Yes.

INTERROGATOR. To *scratch* her to, what? To ... "experiment." To forswear the burden of our stupid lives. To feel the great thrill one can—Yes, one can—derive from ecstatic, unlimited, what? Sex-play, work-play ... life as a ... *(To Assistant.)* Help me out here.

ASSISTANT. *(Pause.)* "Playground."

INTERROGATOR. I don't think so, no. *(Pause.)* Life as a "road accident." As a ... as a depraved revel, eh, of The Last Night of All the World. The last and unobserved instances of humankind. Hid from God's Eye. Free to kill. Free to love, freed from allegiance to this shithole of a life—free to reject it AS IT REJECTS US. Clawing our way back into a realer world. A Death-Pact? "Fucking on a Parapet." *(To Assistant.)* He wanted to shove *what?*

ASSISTANT. A toaster up her ass.

BOB. I didn't *do* it.

INTERROGATOR. No. You *said* it, though. You *said* it. *Did* you...?

BOB. Yes.

INTERROGATOR. Oh, Good! We're *getting* somewhere, then. Two questions, Lad: As you *wanted* to do it, I must ask you, *Had* you done it, would that not have been the act of a Bad Man...

BOB. ... and your second question ...?

INTERROGATOR. What would you have done for toast.

BOB. I could have gone out for toast.

ASSISTANT. Excuse me, excuse me, that was in response to the *second* question...? (*Pause.*)

INTERROGATOR. *Hello,* my Young Champion. (*Pause.*)

ASSISTANT. Hello. (*Pause.*)

INTERROGATOR. What else am I supposed to ask him?

ASSISTANT. Why he led the life he did.

INTERROGATOR. Good boy. (*To Bob.*) Why did you lead the life you did?

BOB. I didn't lead a bad life.

INTERROGATOR. Dint you?

BOB. No.

INTERROGATOR. *Dint* you?

BOB. No.

INTERROGATOR. When you did laundry...?

BOB. What?

INTERROGATOR. When you did "laundry." For others and yourself. In one wash. You commingled the clothes. (*Pause.*) *Did* you not...?

BOB. ... yes ...

INTERROGATOR. In the Wash...

BOB. ... yes. I did.

INTERROGATOR. And then you ... removed the wash. When you "removed" the wash ...

BOB. ...yes ...

INTERROGATOR. ...from the washer...

BOB. ... yes ...

INTERROGATOR. ... did you not ... now answer carefully, now, did you not *inevitably* Take Your Jeans Out First...? (*Pause.*)

BOB. ... yes ...

INTERROGATOR. Indeed. And ... take your jeans out first, thinking thus: "What a swine I am. To act so selfishly ... why am I powerless to leave off this selfish behavior...(*Pause.*) Why... why... why can't I first remove the Jeans of others, why..."

BOB. ...what harm did it do ...?

ASSISTANT. ... the Damned Impertinence ...

INTERROGATOR. Harm.

BOB. Yes.

BOB. ... I ...

INTERROGATOR. What is this, a Laundry? You SINNED.

ASSISTANT. ... sir, you don't have to tell him ...

INTERROGATOR. You elected that it was a sin, THEN YOU COMMITTED IT. You, *you* are the Harm that it did.

BOB. I ...

INTERROGATOR. Your *soul* is the harm it did. The...

BOB. I ...

INTERROGATOR. The undisputed mis'ry in the world is the, eh, "Harm that it did." It is not a "thing," it is not a "breadbox," it's not a "virus," it is you. You. You are the Harm. You "sinner." The State of the World is the Harm That it Did! Bored yet?

BOB. Yes.

INTERROGATOR. Well perhaps this is your punishment.

BOB. Look, look, look. I'm sorry about the jeans...

INTERROGATOR. Yes ...?

BOB. But:
INTERROGATOR. I'm listening.
BOB. I can not say that I am a bad man. (*Pause.*)
INTERROGATOR. Well, then, you just haven't been paying attention.
BOB. No, no. I hear what you're saying, but I just cannot agree with you.
INTERROGATOR. Oh, Lord...
BOB. And I would like to go home.
INTERROGATOR. You can't go home.
BOB. *Why* can't I go home?
INTERROGATOR. Because you were Bad.
BOB. Nothing's black and white.
INTERROGATOR. Nothing's black and white...? NOTHING'S BLACK AND WHITE? ... What about a *Panda*? (*ASSISTANT hands the Devil a large photographic representation of a panda, which the DEVIL displays to Bob and then hands back to the Assistant.*) ... What about a *Panda* ... you Dumb Fuck.
BOB. I ...
INTERROGATOR. What about a fucking *Panda*...? What? Cat Got Your Tongue...?
BOB. ... does the Cat have my Tongue...?
INTERROGATOR. Yes.
BOB. No.
INTERROGATOR. Well. Thank God for Small Mercies. Okay. Okay. C'mon. You just, look here: you just Confess to your, your "wretched Life," and we'll Get On with it.
BOB. I can't do that.
INTERROGATOR. Why not?
BOB. Because ... it Would Not Be Right.
INTERROGATOR. It "Would Not Be Right"...?
BOB. No.

INTERROGATOR. (*Sighs.*) Oh, Lord, we're gonna be here for a while.

ASSISTANT. Tea. Sir?

INTERROGATOR. What?

ASSISTANT. Tea.

INTERROGATOR. Yes. Tea. Yes. Tea for three. Yes. I think so. "I don't think I led such a bad life. And what is real? And how are we to know?" *I* see. (*Pause.*) In a sane world. In a sane, happy little land, in a happy land of light, where all was ordered; trig white picket fences, and yes, yes, the occasional choirmaster violating young boys in the organ loft. That's a part of it, too, isn't it? That's a part of it, too, we have days of sun ... and we have the "grey" days ... (*Sighs. To Bobby.*) I'm sorry ... I assumed you wanted tea.

BOB. I do want tea.

INTERROGATOR. How do you take it?

BOB. White?

INTERROGATOR. How jolly. You see? One with a little milk, and one with lemon. What a mystery. Why we do the things we do. Continually diverting. (*To Bob.*) Waal, All right ... You "flew off the handle." You killed and ate this young girl. You had your provocations ... But, since Man must make an End, we must say you were wrong to "do" it. Weren't cha?

BOB. I didn't actually ...

INTERROGATOR. You didn't actually what?

BOB. I didn't Kill and Eat a Young Girl.

INTERROGATOR. Oh. Oh. Oh well, you must just pardon me I haven't had the time you see, to give your notes the strict attention I am sure they so richly deserve. I beg your understanding. Pardon Me. YOU LED A DEPRAVED LIFE. YOU LED A DEPRAVED LIFE, You did, Laddie. Don't you tell *me* what you did, I'll tell *you*. I'll tell *you*.... What you did and what you *meant*, and what it's going to *cost* you. "You didn't actually..." Fuck with *me*, pal...?

ASSISTANT. (*To Bob. Sotto.*) You're in a lot of trouble ...

INTERROGATOR. Fuck with me...? Eh. Fuck with the lady behind the window at the Auto Registry, you stand a better chance. But Do not FUCK with me. (*To Assistant.*) Forget his tea. I want tea, and you can have tea, but he may not have his tea.

ASSISTANT. I've already poured it, sir.

INTERROGATOR. Well, that's *your* lookout. Now, then. Now: Shall we begin *again*...?

BOB. I would like to make a statement.

INTERROGATOR. Fine. We will consider that your statement.

BOB. No, I would like to make *another* statement.

ASSISTANT. No, you made your statement.

BOB. I ... no, I have something to say.

INTERROGATOR. What's on your mind?

BOB. I tried to live a good life. I'm sure that in some ways ...

ASSISTANT. (*Writing.*) Wait, wait ... "Good life..." all right ... go on ...

BOB. I'm sure that in some ways ...

INTERROGATOR. Yeah, yeah, yeah, in some ways you fell short. That's Why We're HERE today.

BOB. Why are you browbeating me...?

INTERROGATOR. You forfeited any claims on my courtesy when you killed and ate that young girl.

ASSISTANT. ...he didn't actually...

BOB. ...What is it you want of me...?

INTERROGATOR. Tell me why you did the things that you did.

BOB. You want me to "confess."

INTERROGATOR. Well, yes.

BOB. To "confess" to you.

INTERROGATOR. Don't you "want" to? You want to this, to, to ... "that" ... to, to see God. Let's blow the lid off this. Has it occurred to you, in your search for "God," that, perhaps, "I" am God? (*Pause.*) Mmm? Or, perhaps "you" are "God." You want to talk theology ... fine. Fine. Has it occurred to you?

BOB. ... I Just Don't Know.

INTERROGATOR. Come on, then, we're all friends here. Has it occurred to you...? (*Pause.*)

BOB. It has occurred to me that you are God. (*Pause.*)

INTERROGATOR. Oh. Jolly Good!

BOB. It has occurred to me that *I* am God.

INTERROGATOR. ... that you are God. Well, if *you're* God, why don't you just turn me into a Ham Sandwich and *Eat* me. Blows holes in *that* theory, then, *don't* it. Or that we're "*all*" God. That "God" is a spirit. Rampant in the World. In All Things. Full of *Goodness.* "Perfect Knowledge," if you will. Of *what*? Of "Itself." How 'bout that...? N'all of this "shoving toasters up of people's ass," is merely ... what? (*Pause.*) What? (*Pause.*)

ASSISTANT. ... The "frosting on the cake"? (*Pause.*)

INTERROGATOR. No.

BOB. I AM NOT BAD.

INTERROGATOR. Uh huh. Johann Sebastian One-Note. (*Sighs.*) You said you wanted ... "to clean her apartment," "Down to the minutest recesses of ..." one would suppose you meant the 'corners'..."on your knees, dressed in an apron." A "*toothbrush*" supposedly, yes? various *cleansing* powders ... Did you say that?

BOB. Yes.

INTERROGATOR. And yet you persist in denying your desire for purification. And you tell me that you don't want to confess. But you are incapable of uttering that which is not a lie. Aren't you? Everything you have told

me is a lie. IT IS A LIE. And yet you stand mute. Giving
us to understand what? Your defense is ... what? "Human
Nature"... eh? eh? (*Turns to Assistant.*)

ASSISTANT. ... human nature ... (*Pause.*)

INTERROGATOR. (*To Assistant.*) Signifying what...?

ASSISTANT. (*Pause.*) I'm sorry?

INTERROGATOR. You said "human nature." (*Pause.*)

ASSISTANT. Yes.

INTERROGATOR. I said "human nature," and then
"*you*" said "human nature." (*Pause.*) What did you mean
when you said that?

ASSISTANT. ... I was agreeing with you. (*Pause.*)

INTERROGATOR. Uh huh. You know. You can have
a life too. I have a life, You too, can have your own life.
Your Own Wee Life. You can have it.

ASSISTANT. Thank you sir.

INTERROGATOR. You are most welcome. (*To Bob.*)
Now: You wanted to cleanse yourself, Pal. Why would you
want to *cleanse* yourself if you were not unclean? No? All
right. This "girl," for example. You *said* things to her.
You called her your...

ASSISTANT. (*Pause.*) "Honeypie."

INTERROGATOR. You're bluffing.

ASSISTANT. No.

INTERROGATOR. Oh. Yes. You are. Confess it.

BOB. I did call her my honeypie.

INTERROGATOR. You lying and pathetic swine.
Think he can help you? *No* one can help you. YOU ARE
IN DEEP SHIT.

BOB. I didn't treat her bad.

INTERROGATOR. What? "Pencils up, Pally." YOU
CAUSED PAIN. It's not for nothing that we feel
"Compassion." "Conscience." Sense of Right and Wrong.
We have a compass. *You* know when you are doing bad ...
WE know when, you see, me boyo, this is why all

cultures have "religions"... see...? Differing lands, different sides of the Earth...

ASSISTANT. ... that's right

INTERROGATOR. All come up with the Same Rules. Those same, silly rules. The same Gods...the same "rituals." Mumbo This—and Jumbo *That*. The Rain God, the Winter Solstice God, the ...the ...

ASSISTANT. The "fish" God.

INTERROGATOR. The "fish" God, yes ... thank you. Because there is that, is there not, that universal and eternal element in us. Is there not? It is "conscience." It links us to God. And, in regard to it, You've Shit The Bed.

BOB. No. No. I've had enough. Excuse me. I may have done This or That, but on the whole, I have to say, I Was a Good Man! (*BOBBY tries to exit through the double doors again but gets HELLFIRE and SCREAMS again and closes the door and sits down.*)

ASSISTANT. Sir ...?

INTERROGATOR. What?

ASSISTANT. What if we sent him back, but cut his dick off...?

INTERROGATOR. Oh, grow up.

BOB. I WAS A GOOD MAN.

ASSISTANT. What about the time you didn't call your uncle that time when he was so sick...?

BOB. Oh c'mon, we hadn't been speaking for a while, and I really ...

INTERROGATOR. Oh, God, and I wanted to get out of here.

BOB. I Was a Good Man ... The world's a confusing place ... how many "perfect" people are there in it? You tell me that. How many...

INTERROGATOR. Bring the girl down...

BOB. How many "stainless," that's not what I mean, you know what I mean ... how can you sit there and tell me...

INTERROGATOR. Bring the girl down.

(The ASSISTANT consults his book.)

ASSISTANT. ... it will take a moment ...

BOB. You cannot tell me I am worse than the average guy who ...

INTERROGATOR. *(To himself.)* Oh, let's get out of here ...

BOB. ... worse than the average...

INTERROGATOR. I tell you what I'm going to do. Call me a fool. But I'm going to give you a chance. All right? Divine *correctly* the question I now put to you, and you will, that's right, Go Free. No Crossies. Whatcha say?

BOB. I ...

INTERROGATOR. I ask you a question, and if you Guess Right, Then You Go Free.

BOB. Why do you *tantalize* me ...? Why do you tease me? Would it not be kinder to...

INTERROGATOR. ...yes, yes, yes. We get it. We get it. Hey, I made you the offer, you want it or not? Of *course* you want it. Here it is. I say: I'm thinking of a number. Then *you* have to guess, *you* have to guess if I am *really* thinking of a number. *(Pause.)*

BOB. *You* say you're thinking of ...

INTERROGATOR. ... *you* get it.

BOB. And I guess *right*, and I get to Go Back to the World.

INTERROGATOR. Yes.

BOB. And lead a ... lead ... lead a good ... "Lead a Good Life."

INTERROGATOR. You can lead Whatever the Deuce Kind of Life you Like.

BOB. And All I Have to Do is Guess the Number That...

INTERROGATOR. ... no, no ... no you don't have to "guess" the "number." No, *I* say "I'm thinking of a number," and all *you* have to do is guess *whether or not I,* in fact AM ... "Thinking" of a number.

BOB. ... I ...

INTERROGATOR. Or you can Rot in Hell Forever, mired in the unresolvable torments of your Past Life. Think about it.

(GLENNA appears in a puff of smoke. SHE is dressed in a nightgown and holds a toothbrush and a television remote channel changer.)

GLENNA. Where am I?
INTERROGATOR. Hell.
GLENNA. Literally or figuratively?

(INTERROGATOR indicates his horns. HE points at her, the Channel Changer that SHE is holding SPARKS and dissolves in flame..)

GLENNA. Oh!
INTERROGATOR. That's right.
GLENNA. I don't belong here.
INTERROGATOR. Yes, we are aware of that, we only...
GLENNA. I led a ...
INTERROGATOR. ... to be sure...
GLENNA. Good Life.
INTERROGATOR. Yes, we only...
GLENNA. I was thoughtful, I ...

INTERROGATOR. (*To Assistant.*) Explain it to her.

GLENNA. I was mindful, I was, of the suffering of ...

INTERROGATOR. Yes. We brought you down here...

GLENNA. I was a victim. I was a victim.

ASSISTANT. (*Writing.*) "A victim ..."

GLENNA. Yes.

ASSISTANT. (*Writing.*) "Mindful of the suffering..."

GLENNA. I tried to love. I was sinned against.

INTERROGATOR. You tried to love.

GLENNA. Yes.

INTERROGATOR. How is that different from "loving?"

GLENNA. F'you don't know, I can't tell you.

INTERROGATOR. Uh huh. (*To Assistant.*) Hell with it, send her home. Don't need another *victim* down here.

ASSISTANT. We're going to send you home now. (*HE starts to usher her toward the doors.*)

GLENNA. I was good. I was kind. All day. I was helping People. I was a Medical Assistant, I ...

INTERROGATOR. (*To Assistant.*) ONE MOMENT. You were WHAT?

GLENNA. A medical assistant. I ... is that a crr ...

INTERROGATOR. "Is that a Crime...?" "Is that a Crime...?" People Sick With Fear, and you say... "What is it they say?" It is ... (*To Assistant.*) what is it...? What is it...?

ASSISTANT. "Customary" ...

INTERROGATOR. Thank you... "Customary to Pay For Professional Medical Services When Rendered." (*Pause.*) Well?

GLENNA. ... I ...

INTERROGATOR. People under anesthesia. Old, fat women, and you *looked* at the, you looked at their ravaged, jellied thighs. Thighs fairly *running* down their legs, whilst they lay on the table and their... *(Gestures to the ASSISTANT, who checks notes.)*

ASSISTANT. ... stockings

INTERROGATOR. ... were held by these *cheap elastics,* just above their knees. These sick old women, and you thought "Why would you want to live?" Why would you want to live? "You *know* nobody wants to *fuck* you ... why don't you just die...?" Deny it!

ASSISTANT. *(Sotto.)* You are a master, sir ...

INTERROGATOR. Yes. You may *well* cry. Cry for yourself. Eh? Cry for suffering Humanity ... cry for the unabated savagery of ...

GLENNA. ...you're shouting at me.

INTERROGATOR. I am not.

GLENNA. You were.

INTERROGATOR. If I was, then I'm sorry.

GLENNA. Thank you.

INTERROGATOR. Take her to the pit.

ASSISTANT. ... Sir? But we just called her down to ...

INTERROGATOR. I don't care. Take her away to rot in hell for eternity.

GLENNA. ... be ... because of What I Did?

INTERROGATOR. No. Cause I don't like your lipstick.

GLENNA. I ...

INTERROGATOR. *(Pause.)* What?

GLENNA. If I thought that. Of those ladies. Then I'm Sorry.

INTERROGATOR. No doubt.

GLENNA. But...

INTERROGATOR. But what?

GLENNA. ... their thighs were too fat.

INTERROGATOR. Oh, Lord, when things go wrong...

GLENNA. And that's not just my *"opinion"* that's the *truth.*

INTERROGATOR. All right ... all right ... *on* with it ... here we go ... you ...

ASSISTANT. ... the book? (*Pause.*)

INTERROGATOR. ... what?

ASSISTANT. ... the book, Sir?

INTERROGATOR. Yes. Give me the book.

GLENNA. ... I led a life of Suffering and Good. I was Good. I was Betrayed. I did Good, and was mistreated. I ... I don't think the things that I did were that bad.

INTERROGATOR. You don't.

GLENNA. No.

INTERROGATOR. The women. With the fat, fat thighs.

GLENNA. No.

INTERROGATOR. The times you disobeyed your mom?

GLENNA. No.

INTERROGATOR. No? The mixed-race child you scowled at when he wanted a Kind Look.

GLENNA. I never did that.

INTERROGATOR. Yes. You did.

GLENNA. I'd never act that way.

INTERROGATOR. You did it, though.

GLENNA. Did not.

INTERROGATOR. You did, too.

BOB. You *are* thinking of a number.

INTERROGATOR. No. But feel free to try again.

GLENNA. What is he doing here ?

ASSISTANT. Well, that's for us to know, and you to fff...

GLENNA. Why is he here? Why? Is this my punishment? For WHAT? He wronged me on Earth, and he plagues me here ...

INTERROGATOR. ... Ain't that the way.

GLENNA. He told me...

INTERROGATOR. Yes.

GLENNA. That he was going to shove a *toaster* up my ass!

INTERROGATOR. No!

GLENNA. Yes.

INTERROGATOR. Oh Lord, how we have perverted your perfect world.

GLENNA. And...

INTERROGATOR. There's more?

GLENNA. AAAAND ... he screwed me, and he told me he was going to call me, and he never called me up.

INTERROGATOR. *(To Bob.)* Get her to pardon you, you both go free.

GLENNA. I don't *want* him to go free. I want to go free, and I want *him* to Rot in Hell. You *swine*. To get some girl to...lay you, you say...

BOB. ... I never said it

GLENNA. ... if you say you "love" her.

BOB. ... I never said that.

GLENNA. ... you *did*.

BOB. ... I *didn't* ...

GLENNA. The Hell you didn't you DID. *(To Assistant.)* Check the book...

ASSISTANT. ... I ...

GLENNA. ... CHECK THE GODDAMNED BOOK ... and did you think it *amused* me—to be lied to?

ASSISTANT. *(Pause.)* ... Miss ...

GLENNA. Can you think that gave me pleasure? *(Pause.)* What *is* pleasure...? I'm talking to you.

BOB. Um. Pleasure is ... I ... um ... um ... Pleasure is the Absence of Pain.

GLENNA. The Absence of Pain. And that's what we pursue the whole time? The Absence of Pain...?

BOB. Yes.

GLENNA. Is it?

BOB. I don't know.

GLENNA. Well, then, guess. Because I won't stop asking until you have guessed.

BOB. No. I don't know what pleasure is.

GLENNA. Too well-told ... all the things that you've done to me ... (*Of Assistant who is looking at book.*) Did you find where he says it...?

ASSISTANT. No. I ... something, he says I "LLLL"...

GLENNA. Give me that book ... (*Takes book.*) "I love you." Said it several times—somebody's got to pay.

INTERROGATOR. All right. All right. That's the point. Step down. That's the stuff. (*To Bob.*) You see? And that's what you engendered. (*To Glenna.*) Thank you. 'Ppreciate it. (*To Bob.*) You caused that pain, Bob. (*To Glenna.*) You can go now.

GLENNA. I can go?

INTERROGATOR. Yes.

GLENNA. Oh. (*Pause.*) Oh, You're through with me, and so, goodbye. You know. I didn't *ask* to come here.

INTERROGATOR. I know. That's why you can go.

GLENNA. You want me to go?

INTERROGATOR. Yes.

GLENNA. Ask me nicely.

INTERROGATOR. Please go.

GLENNA. Ask me nicely.

INTERROGATOR. I *am* asking you nicely.

GLENNA. You're asking me. But you're not asking me nicely.

INTERROGATOR. I ... I ... I am asking you nicely.

GLENNA. No. You're not.

INTERROGATOR. All right. All right. I'm ... how will I know when I am?

GLENNA. You'll know.

INTERROGATOR. How will I know?

GLENNA. Because you will feel it in your heart.

INTERROGATOR. Aha. But ...

GLENNA. No. There's no "but." You'll feel it.

INTERROGATOR. But, if I "feel" it now...?

GLENNA. Yes. But *now* you're wrong.

INTERROGATOR. How will I know when I'm right?

GLENNA. I'll tell you.

INTERROGATOR. Aha. (*To Assistant.*) If you have ever loved me. Get her out of here.

ASSISTANT. Ask her to leave, sir.

INTERROGATOR. I have asked her to leave, but she will not leave.

ASSISTANT. (*Checking book.*) Apparently she's free to leave or stay, sir, as she's down here as a guest.

INTERROGATOR. ... As a guest ... Fuck me I'm a poodle. Look, look, I'm trying to get *out* of here.

GLENNA. Well that's your choice then, isn't it?

INTERROGATOR. And I'd like you to leave.

GLENNA. Have I done something to *offend* someone? (*Pause.*) Because if I have, you understand...? Tell me, and I'll *address* it. (*Pause.*) LET'S JUST ... HAVE THE COURTESY, IF I'VE DONE SOMETHING NOT QUITE TO YOUR TASTE ... to *tell* me rather than ... *Internalize* this, this, this ... this (*To Bobby.*) and you were like this too ... (*Generally.*) *Neurotic need to feel wronged.* Life is too short. You know? And it's not *acts* that matter—you could do the seemingly most friendly action in a ... in a *snide* or *hidden* way, and what is that but hate? Hate and self-*loathing*. So ... so ... where was I...?

INTERROGATOR. I have it in my power to render you the office of the Queen of Time. And all things Earthly and ethereal will be yours. All things. For the body and the soul. The power to Call the Winds. To Move the Mountains—to Command the Living and the Dead. Riches and majesty untold...

GLENNA.   And why don't *I*, why don't *I* have the power to award *you* those things? DO YOU SEE? HOW INCREDIBLY "DEMEANING" THAT IS? Who Died and Left *You* The Boss? (*SHE looks at the book.*) Here it is: "I LOVE YOU."

(*Shows the book to Bobby. HE looks at the book.*)

BOB. That is not an "L."
GLENNA. ... It is not an "L"?
BOB. No.
GLENNA. What *is* it, then? Pick something more *worthy* of you. You understand? ... and you said it again on ... (*To Assistant, of book.*) Find it.
ASSISTANT. ... Miss ...?
GLENNA. Find it for me.
ASSISTANT. ... I ...
GLENNA. ... one morning. We were having coffee. Something just happened in Asia. It was on the News. This sonofabitch. Said "I Love You." Find it.
ASSISTANT. (*Reading in book.*) Ah. Sir! Sir!
GLENNA. (*To Interrogator.*) You see ...?
ASSISTANT. (*Reading the book.*) Here we actually have an *instance* of Two Jewish Gentlemen who went into a bar. (*Pause.*) One of them asks for a libation of some sort...
GLENNA. I'm sorry ...?
ASSISTANT. These two Jews go into a bar ...
GLENNA. Yes?
ASSISTANT. They go into a bar, and ...
GLENNA. Yes?
ASSISTANT. One asks the other if he'd like a *drink* ...
GLENNA. (*Takes the book, reads.*) "I cannot join you, for today is the Feast Of..."

INTERROGATOR. Hey, Hey, Hey. I HAVE TO *WORK* HERE. WHAT IS YOUR *PROBLEM*? I HAVE TO WORK DOWN HERE.

GLENNA. (*Reading from book.*) "the two renowned Talmudic Scholars then *left* the bar ..." (*The Interrogator points at the book. The book bursts into FLAMES.*)

INTERROGATOR. Look, okay, I've had a Bad Day.

GLENNA. I was reading I believe...?

INTERROGATOR. I've had a bad day, and ...

GLENNA. Well, that's just unfortunate, but, you see, I'd be betraying *myself* if I let you play upon my sympathy.

INTERROGATOR. (*To Assistant.*) Get. Her. Out. Of. Here.

GLENNA. ... *you* see that ...

INTERROGATOR. Here is my last ... (*To Assistant.*) Do I have the power to do this ...?

ASSISTANT. ... Sir.

INTERROGATOR. Here ... is my last offer.

GLENNA. I'll be the judge of what is whose last offer.

INTERROGATOR. (*Pause.*) If you'll go home, I'll pardon all humanity.

GLENNA. (*Pause.*) What am I ... cattle? That you think you can trade on ... trade, trade on my *emotions*?

ASSISTANT. People do not trade on the emotions of cattle.

GLENNA. ... Do you think you can ...

INTERROGATOR. I will absolve all Humanity of All crimes ...

GLENNA. If I will "what?" *I DON'T DEAL.* I don't "negotiate," I, and I take this, yes, I heard you, this "appeal," to my ... "Altruism," to my fellow-feeling, as, I'm sorry, but I'm going to say it, as "manipulative."

INTERROGATOR. GET OUT OF HERE!!! GET OUT OF HERE!!! WHAT HAVE I DONE??? I'M A BUSY MAN!!!

GLENNA. A busy man?

INTERROGATOR. Yes.

GLENNA. You are nothing to me but your actions towards me on an particular day. You see? (*Pause.*)

INTERROGATOR. Yes.

GLENNA. You see?

INTERROGATOR. Yes.

GLENNA. I would like to think you see ... but I have to trust my perceptions.

INTERROGATOR. ... of course.

GLENNA. Don't mollify me.

INTERROGATOR. I wasn't.

GLENNA. You were.

INTERROGATOR. If I was I'm sorry.

GLENNA. I don't require you to be sorry.

INTERROGATOR. No. Of course not.

GLENNA. What do you mean "of course not"?

INTERROGATOR. I meant you were right.

GLENNA. I was right.

INTERROGATOR. Yes.

GLENNA. When I said "what?" (*Pause.*)

INTERROGATOR. I ... I don't remember.

GLENNA. Why do you "toy" with me?

INTERROGATOR. ... toy with you.

GLENNA. Yes.

INTERROGATOR. I don't know.

GLENNA. Uh huh ... (*Pause.*) And ... and do you ever think, then, why you perform in ways you cannot account for? (*Pause.*)

INTERROGATOR. I ...

GLENNA. Have you ever thought about *counselling?* (*Pause.*) Have you?

INTERROGATOR. Well, I ...

GLENNA. I mean *seriously.* Seriously. Ever thought about *making that commitment?* (*Pause.*)

INTERROGATOR. I will.

GLENNA. No, I mean seriously.

INTERROGATOR. Yes. Yes.

(*BOBBY GOULD comes over. Claps him lightly on the shoulder.*)

BOB. (*Sotto.*) I'm with you ...

GLENNA. ... Because, you know, these things in our life: we needn't be *ruled* by them. But our *Spirits* are a *closed system.* Y'understand? You can't act one way during the day, and, and not expect it to ... to ...

ASSISTANT. ... reflect ...?

GLENNA. Was I speaking to you? (*To Interrogator.*) ... reflect on what transpires at night, to ... to *express* itself in your ... in your ... nobody help me, now ... in your ... in ...what was I talking about? In your relationships.

INTERROGATOR. Yes.

GLENNA. Do you see?

INTERROGATOR. Yes.

GLENNA. Do you see how far we got when we can just be *reasonable?*

INTERROGATOR. Mmm. (*Pause.*) You know, Bob ... Bob has "lost his soul"...

BOB. (*To himself.*) What...?

GLENNA. Well, Bob, I told you it was going to happen.

BOB. You did.

GLENNA. Didn't I?

BOB. ... Yes.

GLENNA. That night in the restaurant ...

BOB. You did.

GLENNA. Why did you talk to the waiter that way?
BOB. I'm sorry.
GLENNA. You see what it *got* you.
BOB. Yes. (*Pause.*)

(*GLENNA sighs.*)

INTERROGATOR. And the ...
GLENNA. (*Simultaneously with "And the."*) We ...
INTERROGATOR. I ... Did I interrupt your train of...?
GLENNA. No. No. (*Pause.*) You were saying?
INTERROGATOR. I was saying that there is a ... do you know, because you've *moved* me. With you "thoughts"...
GLENNA. It's ... it's so simple, really.
INTERROGATOR. Yes. Mmm. And it made me reflect that there is a substantial "bulk" of religious opinion to the effect that ...
GLENNA. ...that ...
INTERROGATOR. That the *Highest Good* ...
GLENNA. Yes. I know. You want me to be gone. You want me to pardon *Bob,* who professed "love" for me, and then Broke My Heart. Yes. I know. And you see that heartbreak doesn't stop. It's *with* me, you see, every moment. When I see a "chair," ... or Every moment.
INTERROGATOR. Yes, I'm sorry.
GLENNA. And how many moments *are* there in a day...?
INTERROGATOR. How many ...
GLENNA. Yes. For Good or Ill. How many moments when ...
INTERROGATOR. I think I'm thinking of a number...
GLENNA. Are you being flip with me ...? What did he say?
INTERROGATOR. I said I'm thinking of a number.

GLENNA. (*To Interrogator.*) No, you aren't. (*SHE
vanishes in a puff of SMOKE.*)

INTERROGATOR. Yes, yes, yes, yes, yes. There's
nothing like technique. Frolicsome little bint.

BOB. Can I go home now?

INTERROGATOR. What?

BOB. Can I go now?

INTERROGATOR. Oh, Lordy, me, I *do* enjoy a jest!
Why would you think you can go home? (*Pause.*)

BOB. She proved my point.

INTERROGATOR. What point is that?

BOB. My *point* ...

INTERROGATOR. ... present it ...

BOB. That I am not a bad man. All right. All right.
That *she* was impossible. She was impossible. *You* saw it.
SHE DROVE ME MAD. She was impossible. There was
no pleasing her. I did my best.

INTERROGATOR. She like that when you *met* her?

BOB. No. Yes.

INTERROGATOR. Which is it? Eh? *Whichever* one.
You sure dint *help* her, any, *didja? Didja?* What's the book
say? Whad'd he do...?

ASSISTANT. (*Checking the book.*) "Treated her
shoddily."

INTERROGATOR. "Treated her shoddily." That fair...?

BOB. I don't *know* what's fair. I don't care, what the
"book" says, I don't care what you say. I don't care what it
costs me. I am not going to sit here and say I was a Bad
Man. You understand? I am not going to do it. I have to
have my pride, I *do* have a life, and I have a vision of the
world, and it may be right or it may *not*, but it is mine. I
am not a Bad Man. I'm going now. (*Pause.*) I am not a Bad
Man. (*BOBBY opens the double doors to find HELLFIRES
and a BEAR. HE grapples with the BEAR, escapes, slams
the doors and sits down.*)

(Pause.)

INTERROGATOR. Oh, all right.

BOB. What do you mean?

INTERROGATOR. I mean "all right." I give up. I'm done.

BOB. What do you mean that you're done?

INTERROGATOR. I mean I give up. I'm goin' fishin'.

(Pause.)

BOB. What do *I* do?

INTERROGATOR. Go home.

BOB. What do you mean "go home"?

INTERROGATOR. I mean you win. Go home.

(Pause.)

BOB. You mean it?

INTERROGATOR. Here's my hand on it.

BOB. What about my being a "Bad Man"?

INTERROGATOR. Being a "Bad Man." Forget it. You can be whatever you say you are.

BOB. You mean it?

INTERROGATOR. Yes, I do.

BOB. The Game's Over?

INTERROGATOR. The game is over and you win.

BOB. Oli Oli in come free?

INTERROGATOR. You stickler.

BOB. Say it.

INTERROGATOR. Oli Oli in come free.

(THEY shake hands.)

ASSISTANT. *(Writing.)* ... in come free.

INTERROGATOR. I want to tell you something. I know that it's rough.

BOB. ... it's rough ...?

INTERROGATOR. Life is rough.

BOB. *That's* too well-told.

INTERROGATOR. It's tough to know what to do.

BOB. Yes. To know what to do, and then do it ...

INTERROGATOR. Yes. That's right.

BOB. And, then, we're only human ...

INTERROGATOR. That's right.

BOB. And we all fail, sometimes.

INTERROGATOR. Don't we ...

BOB. Yes, we do.

INTERROGATOR. We don't mean to.

BOB. No.

INTERROGATOR. But we do. I know that the world is a cruel place. Isn't it?

BOB. Yes, it is.

ASSISTANT. (*Hands him a form.*) Sign here.

INTERROGATOR. And, many times, we Do Not Know what's right.

BOB. You know many things ... *don't* you ...?

INTERROGATOR. I know life hurts.

BOB. It does hurt.

INTERROGATOR. And, I know that if it were "given" to us, to "salve" that hurt.

BOB. To salve that hurt.

INTERROGATOR. We would do anything. (*Pause.*) Would we not?

BOB. We would.

INTERROGATOR. And ... many times ... we want to call out "*Show* me God ..." "*Let* me Do Good ..."

BOB. ... for who wants to cause pain ...?

INTERROGATOR. *No* one. *No* one desires to Cause Pain.

BOB. No.

INTERROGATOR. (*Hands a form to Bob.*) This is your release.

BOB. Thank you.

INTERROGATOR. And we feel, if we could go back ... we could *atone*, you see, through *purity* ... through knowing the way. Through the Pure Perfection of Our Acts.

BOB. Our Acts. Yes.

INTERROGATOR. That we would Walk in Love ...

BOB. Well, yes, of *course* we would.

INTERROGATOR. In accordance with that constancy, that Constant Principle, which we must feel is God.

(*Pause.*)

BOB. You know that all these things are true.

INTERROGATOR. Yes. But we *cannot* so act, now. Can we?

BOB. No.

INTERROGATOR. *Why* not?

BOB. What? *I* don't know.

INTERROGATOR. Mmm.

BOB. You know, I think, I think, that it's a lack of self-esteem.

INTERROGATOR. Mmm ...

BOB. People feel ...

INTERROGATOR. ...Yes?

BOB. They feel "*bad.*"

INTERROGATOR. ...Yes ...?

BOB. ... they feel bad, and so they "act" bad. (*Pause.*)

INTERROGATOR. Why do they feel bad, Bob?

BOB. I don't know.

INTERROGATOR. ... Mmm.

BOB. They feel that they have "sinned."

INTERROGATOR. They cannot be forgiven, becuase they have *sinned.*

BOB. Yes.

INTERROGATOR. Inn't that something...?

BOB. Umm. (*Pause.*)

INTERROGATOR. *Why* do we sin, Bob? You're an intelligent man ... Why do you think we sin? (*Pause.*)

BOB. I think ...

INTERROGATOR. Yes?

BOB. I think, and I'm going to tell you ... I think we're lonely.

INTERROGATOR. Lonely?

BOB. I think we want God to notice us.

INTERROGATOR. Really?

BOB. I think that it's no more complex than that.

(*Pause.*)

INTERROGATOR. Shithole of a world.

BOB. Well, that's the world we're born into. Aren't we?

INTERROGATOR. Yes.

BOB. And Human Nature is a *part* of it, *isn't* it?

INTERROGATOR. Yes. It is.

BOB. And that's our nature. (*Pause.*) Difficult world.

INTERROGATOR. *Innit* ...?

BOB. Yes.

(*ASSISTANT pours drinks for the two.*)

INTERROGATOR. Wouldn't it be wonderful. If all the cruelty ... all the pain we see ... if we could, somehow ...

BOB. ... yes ...

INTERROGATOR. Just Say a Magic Word. If all the *suffering* ... You, Bob ... all the things you've seen ... The things which you regret ... (*Raises glass.*) Down Under!

BOB. (*Raises glass.*) Up for Air!

INTERROGATOR. *You* understand ...

BOB. Yes.

INTERROGATOR. Wouldn't it be wonderful, if they had never happened. (*Pause.*) If, in effect, you'd just "dreamed" them, and you could return, and, not only not have done them, but *learn* from them.

BOB. Oh, my God.

INTERROGATOR. Now, wouldn't that be ...

BOB. Yes. (*Pause.*) That would be wonderful. That would be Peace on Earth.

INTERROGATOR. Yes. Yes. Yes. Yes. Yes. (*Pause.*) Do it.

BOB. What?

INTERROGATOR. Do it. You can go back. Whatever you regret, whatever pain you would like to erase. It never happened.

BOB. I don't understand.

INTERROGATOR. Yes, you do. (*Pause.*) You can go back. It never happened.

BOB. ... it never happened...

INTERROGATOR. No.

BOB. The bad things in my life.

INTERROGATOR. No.

BOB. I ... "dreamed" them...?

INTERROGATOR. ... if you will.

BOB. I go back and ... what?

INTERROGATOR. You never were unkind. In your acts or thought. You never wished to be cruel. You never *were* cruel. You were kind. You get the picture...?

BOB. I ...

INTERROGATOR. That's right ... that's right. Nothing that you regret, nothing that you are ashamed of, none of it occurred.

BOB. None of it ever happened.

INTERROGATOR. No.

BOB. There is a what, there is an order in the world I cannot understand. But if I believe that you can "send me back," then ...

INTERROGATOR. ... you don't have to believe it.

BOB. Then what? There exists that mechanism AS IN A DREAM, AND IT NEVER HAPPENED!

INTERROGATOR. Yes.

BOB. MY CRUEL LIFE.

INTERROGATOR. Yes.

BOB. I can go back and, all I have to say is "yes."

INTERROGATOR. That's right.

BOB. And I am ... What? I am what ... "good"...?

INTERROGATOR. If you will.

BOB. Why me?

INTERROGATOR. Why not?

BOB. No, why me?

INTERROGATOR. Why not you?

BOB. You're saying: I can go back, and "right the wrongs," such as they are, of my life, and ... what? Alleviate "sorrow," "cruelty..."

INTERROGATOR. If you will ...

BOB. Why me?

INTERROGATOR. Well, Bob, sometimes it just happens, that we're in one place, at one time, and...

BOB. Oh, please.

INTERROGATOR. I'm sorry ...?

BOB. Why would you give me this power?

INTERROGATOR. ... well ...

BOB. *Why*? (*Pause.*) In Return For What?

INTERROGATOR. For nothing.

BOB. *Spare* me, is what I'm saying. You say "go back, I give you Power to Do Good." And I say: why would you do that?

INTERROGATOR. Call it an act of whimsy.

BOB. Bullshit.

INTERROGATOR. Well, pardon my French.

BOB. No, Bullshit. Please: one thing I learned on the Earth. If it looks Too Good to be True—it's not true. I go back and "Do Good" ... what does it *cost* me?

INTERROGATOR. Nothing.

BOB. All right, then, what's in it for you?

INTERROGATOR. Nothing ... look, I've really got to go. Do you want to *accept* my ...?

BOB. Okay, okay, let me put it ... I don't *know* if I want to accept your offer. Let me put it to you like *this*: I know what you give me if I *do* accept your offer ...

INTERROGATOR. ... I give you...?

BOB. Yes, yes, the power To Do Good, and Universal Love. What do you give me if I *don't*?

INTERROGATOR. You're askimg me seriously ...?

BOB. Absolutely. You say "Go Do Good" ... I want to know What I get if I Don't. (*Pause.*) Oh, my God, I just lost my soul. (*Pause.*) Didn't I ...? I just lost my soul.

INTERROGATOR. Yes. (*The INTERROGATOR shoots a FLAME at Bobby which ignites the Release.*) You see, Bob? You are a Bad Man. (*The INTERROGATOR prepares to leave.*)

BOB. I am a Bad Man.

INTERROGATOR. Yes.

BOB. How bad was I?

INTERROGATOR. You were cruel, without being interesting.

ASSISTANT. (*Writing.*) "Lost his soul." You know. Sometimes it seems like one moment can last forever. (*Pause.*) But years go by ... they ... (*Pause.*) What did I say about the Other One? Mo ... moments "go by slowly" ...?

INTERROGATOR. Yes.

ASSISTANT. ... and years (*Pause.*) Years go by (*Pause.*) And they ... they ... "Flow"—they don't "Flow," ... they ... something. And all the trials ... the things that we do ... all the things we do, they, sometimes ... it seems aas if they ... it's not as if they "happen all at once," but ... but they do, it seems. The cruelty. The things we cannot communicate. The orders of misunderstanding we ... we really "glimpse" them, don't we? We see them. As "spirits," as ... as "thoughts" ... and we turn away. Because we say ... (*Pause.*) We say: "I do not wish to know anymore." (*Pause.*) And know that we are dying, and ... what was I asking? And yet we are called to forgive. (*Pause.*) Aren't we?

INTERROGATOR. What? Oh, piss off. We don't want to hear it. See you. Sorry I was late. For what's it's worth. (*Looks around the room.*) Well, you "buck up" now, you bad, bad man.

BOB. (*To himself.*) I am a Bad Man.

INTERROGATOR. Told you. Goodbye then, little lad. Goodbye all. I'm off. (*To Assistant.*) You close up?

ASSISTANT. Yes, sir.

INTERROGATOR. I'm going to kill some fish. (*INTERROGATOR vanishes.*)

BOB. I suppose I'm going to be down here a while.

ASSISTANT. Mmm.

BOB. Have you been down here long? (*Pause.*) Have you been down here long?

ASSISTANT. Yes.

BOB. I'm a bad man. (*Pause.*)

ASSISTANT. That must be difficult to live with.

BOB. I've ruined everything I ever touched.

ASSISTANT. You did?

BOB. Yes.

ASSISTANT. Why?

BOB. I had a vision of myself as "good."

ASSISTANT. Mmm.

BOB. And, so, whatever evil I did, whatever I did, I told myself it was the act of a Good Man.

ASSISTANT. Uh huh.

BOB. And, so, I didn't see it. (*Pause*.) Isn't that something...? (*Pause*.) Isn't that something, now ...?

ASSISTANT. Well, you learn something new every day.

BOB. Mmm.

ASSISTANT. Why did you do it, then? Do you know why...? (*Pause*.)

BOB. I don't know. (*Pause*.) I don't know anymore.

ASSISTANT. Mmm.

BOB. I don't know why I acted the way I did. But I'm so sorry.

ASSISTANT. (*Writing in his book*.) "I'm so sorry ... (*To Bob*.) Yes. That's it. It is my duty to inform you that you can go home now.

BOB. What?

ASSISTANT. You can go home.

BOB. "Go Home"?

ASSISTANT. You're free to go.

BOB. Why? I don't understand.

ASSISTANT. You don't have to understand, you may go now.

BOB. But, I'm "bad."

ASSISTANT. ... nonetheless ...

BOB. I can Go Home.

ASSISTANT. Yes. (*Pause*.)

BOB. I'm going to Go Home now.

ASSISTANT. Goodbye.

BOB. Oh, yes! Oh, yes! Goodbye. Goodbye. Goodbye to Hell. Goodbye to Guilt! Goodbye to ... Yes. Goodbye. *Thank* you!

ASSISTANT. You are very welcome.

BOB. (*Exits. Reenters*.) Before I go, though, I need to say something ... (*Pause*.)

ASSISTANT. I'm sorry ...?

BOB. I need to say something ...

ASSISTANT. Yes, all right, what do you need to say?

BOB. I need to say that I am *changed.*...

ASSISTANT. You're changed?

BOB. Yes, and I see ... that I've come to see—perhaps through consciousness raised through my sufferings down here—that I see now, that "Goodness"...

ASSISTANT. Yes?

BOB. That real humanity can come only through suffering, That none of us is perfect. But all of us are human, and, that real humanity ...

INTERROGATOR. (*Appearing.*) Hey, the guy said "Go Home" are you *deaf*? Geddoudahere! Shoo. (*Turns to audience.*) And the rest of you folks, I'll catch you later.

End of Play

THE DEVIL AND
BILLY MARKHAM

The Devil and Billy Markham premiered at Lincoln Center in December, 1989 with Dennis Locorriere as the Storyteller, under the direction of Gregory Mosher, with setting by John Lee Beatty, costumes by Jane Greenwood, lighting by Kevin Rigdon, sound by Bill Dreisbach, and illusionist effects by George Schindler.

THE DEVIL AND
BILLY MARKHAM

*The STORYTELLER enters. HE wears a ratty topcoat,
baggy pants, unmatching vest, wrinkled shirt and
spotted necktie. HE carries a mop and a bucket. HE sets
down the bucket and begins to mop floor, humming to
himself. HE looks up—surprised to see the audience.
HE realizes his opportunity. HE smiles. He begins to
recite.*

The Devil walked into Linebaugh's on a rainy Nashville
   night.
While the lost souls sat and sipped their soup in the sickly
   yellow neon light.
And the Devil he looked around the room, and he got down
   on one knee.
He says, "Is there one among you scum who'll roll the dice
   with me?"
Red, he just strums his guitar, pretending not to hear.
And Eddie, he just looks away and takes another sip of
   beer.
Vince, he says, "Not me, I'll pass, I've had my share of
   Hell."
And kept scribbling on a napkin, some song he was sure
   would sell.
Ronnie just kept whisperin' low to the snuff queen who
   clutched at his sleeve.
And somebody coughed—and the Devil scoffed.
And turned on his heel to leave.
"Hold on," says a voice from the back of the room.

"'Fore you walk out that door.
If you're looking for some action friend, well I've rolled
some dice before."
And there stood Billy Markham, he'd been on the scene for
years,
Singing all those raunchy songs that the town didn't want
to hear.
He'd been cut and bled a thousand times, and his eyes were
wise and sad. And all his song were songs of the street,
and all of his luck was bad.
"I know you," says Billy Markham, "from many a dark and
funky place,
But you always spoke in a different voice and wore a
different face.
While me, I've gambled here on Music Row with hustlers,
hacks and whores
And my dues are paid I ain't afraid to roll them dice of
yours."
"Well then get down," says the Devil, "and put that guitar
away,
And take these dice in your luckless hands and I'll tell you
how this game is played.
You get one roll—and you bet your soul—and if you roll
thirteen you win.
And all the joys of flesh and gold are yours to touch and
spend. But if that thirteen don't come up, then kiss your
ass goodbye,
And will your useless bones to God, 'cause your goddamn
soul is mine."
"Thirteen?" says Billy Markham. "Hell, I've played in
tougher games.
I've loved ambitious women and I've rode on wheelless
trains.
So gimme room, you stinkin' fiend, and let it all unwind,

Nobody's ever rolled a thirteen yet, but this just might be
the time."
Then Billy Markham, he takes the dice, and the dice feel
heavy as stones,
"They should," the Devil says, "'cause they're carved outa
Jesus' bones!"
And Billy Markham turns the dice and the dice they have
no spots.
"I'm sorry," says the Devil, "but they're the only ones I
got."
"Well shit," says Billy Markham. "Now I really don't mean
to bitch,
But I never thought I'd stake my roll in a sucker's game
like this."
"Well then walk off," says the Devil. "Nobody's tied you
down."
"Walk off where?" says Billy. It's the only game in town.
But I just wanna say 'fore I make my play, that if I should
chance to lose,
I will this guitar to some would-be star who'll play some
honest blues.
Who ain't afraid to sing the words like damn or shit or
fuck,
And who ain't afraid to put his ass on the stage where he
makes his bucks.
But if he plays this guitar safe, and sings some sugary lies,
I'll haunt him till we meet in Hell—now gimme them
fuckin' dice.
And Billy Markham shakes the dice and yells, "C'mon ...
thirteen,
And the dice they roll—and they come up—blank.
"You lose!" the Devil screams.
But I really must say 'fore we go our way that I really do
like your style,

Of all the fools I've played and beat, you're the first one
    who lost with a smile."
"Well I'll tell you somethin'," Billy Markham says.
"Those odds weren't too damn bad. In fourteen years on
    Music Row, that's the best damn chance I've had."
Then the Devil takes Billy under his cloak, and they walk
    out through Linebaugh's door,
Leavin' Billy's old guitar there on the sawdust floor.
And if you go to Linebaugh's you can see it there today.
Hangin' ... from a nail on that wall of peelin' gray ...
Billy Markham's old guitar ...
That nobody dares to play.

BILLY MARKHAM AND THE FLY

Billy Markham slowly turns on a white hot steel spit,
And his skin it crackles like a roasting pork, and his flesh
    is seared and split,
And sulphur fills his nostrils and he's fed on slime and
    mud.
By a hairy imp with a pointed stick who bastes him in
    spider's blood,
And his eyeballs boil up inside his skull and his throat's
    too charred to scream.
So he sleeps the sleep of the burning dead and he dreams
    unspeakable dreams.
Then in walks the Devil, puttin' little screaming skulls as
    the bells of Hell start clangin',
And his last shot rolls right up to Billy Markham's toes
    And he says, "Hey Bill, how're they hangin?
I'm sorry we couldn't give you a tomb with a view, but
    right now this is the best we got.

But as soon as we're done with Attila the Hun, we'll move
   you right into his spot.
Have you met your neighbors? Have you heard them
   scream? Do they keep you awake in the fire?
Hey, a little more brimstone on number nine—and hoist
   up them thumbs a bit higher.
Ah, you can't get good help these days, Bill, and there ain't
   much profit in Hell,
No, turn that adultress upside down—do I have to do
   everything myself?
I tell you, Bill, it's a full-time job, tending these red hot
   coals,
And all this shovelin' and stokin', fryin' and smokin',
   prodin' and pokin', stretchin' and chokin', why I hardly
   got time for collecting new souls.
Which brings me to the subject of my little visit, now
   you're one of them natural born gamblin' men,
And I'll bet you'd give most anything to get those dice in
   your hands again.
So instead of swimming in this muck and slime and
   burning crisp as (*Tastes him.*) toast...
I'll trade you one roll ... of the dice for the souls ... of the
   ones who love you most."
"Trade the souls of the ones who love me most? Not a
   chance in Hell I will."
"Spoken like a hero," the Devil says. "Hey a little more
   fire for Bill."
"You can roast me bake me or boil me, says Billy.
Go and have your fiendish fun.
A coward dies a thousand times—a brave man dies but
   once."
"Oh beautiful, sensitive, and poetic too, says the Devil
But life ain't like no rhyme.
And I know ways to make a brave man die a million
   times."

"Hey take your shot ... Throw what you got ... But I won't
trade love away."

"That's what they all say," laughs the Devil ... "but when I
turn up the fire, they play."

Then the flame burns white and Bill's flesh burns black and
he smells his roasting stink.

And the hell rats nibble upon his nose ... and Billy begins
to think.

He thinks about his sweetheart who loved him through his
crazy days.

He thinks of his gray-haired momma, hell, she's gettin old
anyway.

He thinks of his baby daughter—He ain't seen her since
last fall.

Then he thinks about walkin' the Earth again and he thinks
of the horrible pain he's in, and he thinks of the game
that he just might win and he yells, "Hey—take 'em
all."

And—Zap—He's back again at Linebaugh's, kneeling on
that same old floor.

And across from him the Devil squats

Ready to play once more.

"I guess my point is still thirteen?" Billy Markham asks.

"The point's the same," the Devil sneers. "But the stakes
are your loved one's ass."

"Well, one never knows," Billy Markham says, "when lady
luck's gonna smile on a man.

And if a charcoal corpse from hell can't roll thirteen, then
who the hell can?"

And Billy Markham shakes the dice and whispers, "Please,
thirteen."

And the dice roll out a ... six ... and a ... six ... and then,
as if in a dream ...

A buzzing fly from a plate nearby, like a messenger sent
from heaven,

Shits—right in the middle of one of them sixes—and turns
    it into a seven.
"Thirteen! Thirteen! Thirteen! Thirteen! I have beat the
    Devil 's play."
"Oh have you now?" the Devil says, and WHOOSH he
    blows that speck away.
"Which only proves," the Devil says, "that hell's too big
    to buck,
And when you're gambling for your ass, don't count on
    flyshit luck."
"Well, Luck and Love ..." sighs Billy Markham, "they
    never do last for long,
But y'know that fly shittin' on that die would have made
    one hell of a song."
"You're a songwriting, fool," the Devil grins. "There ain't
    no doubt about it.
As soon as you go and lose one damn game, you wanna
    write a song about it.
But there's a whole lot more to life and death than the
    rhymes and tunes you give 'em.
And any fool can sing the blues, (*Sings.*) any fool can sing
    the blues, any fool can sing the blues, let's see if you
    can live 'em."
Then—Zap!—Billy wakes up back in hell, bein' stuffed
    with white hot coals.
While imps dance on his head and shit in his hair and wipe
    their asses with his soul ...
And he hears the screams of his momma as she turns in the
    purple flame.
And he hears the cries of his baby girl as she pays the price
    of his game.
He hears the voice of his own true love laugh like a child
    at play,
As she satisfies the Devil in her own sweet lovin' way.

And buzzin 'cross Bill's burnin' bones and landing on his
    starin' eye,
And nibblin on his roastin' flesh is the grinnin'
    Linebaugh's fly.

BILLY MARKHAM'S LAST ROLL

"Good Morning, Billy Markham, it's time to rise and
    shine."
The Devil's word come grindin' into Billy's burnin' mind.
And he opens up one bloodshot eye to that world of living
    death.
And he feels the Devil's bony claw and he smells his rotten
    breath.
"Wake up Sunshine!" the Devil laughs. "I'm giving you
    another turn."
"I'm turning now," Billy Markham growls. "Go away and
    let me burn."
"Well, you sure are a grouch when you wake up, but you
    wouldn't let a chance go by,"
"Another chance to roll thirteen? Hey, stick it where your
    fire don't shine.
I've played your game, now I feel the shame, as I hear my
    loved ones' cries,
And I'll piss on your shoe, if ever you, come near me again
    with them flyshit dice."
"Dice? Dice? Who said dice? Anybody hear me say dice?
Hey, imp, pour my buddy here a cool glass of water and
    throw in a nice big chunk of ice."
"And since when," says Billy, "do you go around handing
    out gifts,
Except pokes from your burning pitchfork or bucketfulls of
    boiling shit?"

"Well, it's Christmas," says the Devil, "and all of us down
    here below,
We sort of celebrate in our own special way, and this year
    you're the star of the show.
Why, just last night I was up on Earth and I seen that
    lovers' moon,
And I said to myself, 'Hey, I bet ol' Billy could use a little
    bit of poon.'"
"Poon?" says Billy Markham. "Last thing I need is poon.
Talk about gettin' my ashes hauled, hell, I'll be all ashes
    soon."
"Damn! Damn! Damn," cries the Devil, "He's been too
    long on the fire.
I told you imps to fry him slow, now you gone and burned
    out his desire.
You gotta leave 'em some hope, leave 'em some dreams,
    so they know what hell is for,
Cause when a man forgets how sweet love is, well, Hell
    ain't Hell no more.
So just to refresh your memory, Billy, we're gonna send
    you back to Earth,
And I'll throw in a little Christmas blessing to remind you
    what life is worth.
For exactly thirteen hours, you can screw who you want to
    screw.
And there ain't no creature on God's Green Earth who is
    gonna say no to you.
While me and all these burning souls and all my imps and
    fiends,
We're gonna sit down here and watch you on that big 24-
    inch color screen.
And we'll see each hump you're humpin', and we'll hear
    each grunt you groan,
And we'll laugh like hell at the look upon your face when
    it's time to come back home."

"Well, a chance is a chance is a chance," says Billy,
  steppin' down off the sizzlin' coals.
"But what if one won't gimme none, what if one says
  'no'?"
"No? What if one says 'no'? Ain't nobody gonna say 'no.'
Nobody quits or calls in sick when the Devil calls the
  show.
Not man nor woman nor beast!," shouts the Devil. "And
  no laters or maybes or buts,
And before one soul says no to you I will see these Hell
  gates rust.
But ... if any one refuses you, I say, any one you name,
Then you'll be free to stay on Earth, now get out and play
  the game!"
Then a flash of light ... and a thunderclap ... and Billy's
  back on Earth once more,
And the asphalt sings beneath his feet as he swings toward
  Music Row.
First he stops in at the Exit Inn to seduce the blond on the
  door,
Then the RCA receptionist he takes on the office floor.
He nails the waitress down at Mack's, the one with the
  pear-shaped breasts, and four of the girls from B.M.I.
  right on Frances Preston's desk.
He screws his way from M.C.A. to Vanderbilts ivy walls,
And he pokes everything that giggles or sings or whimpers
  or wiggles or crawls
First Debbie, then Polly, then Dotty, then Dolly, then
  Jeannie, and Jessie and Jan,
 Then Marshall and Sal and that red-headed gal who takes
  the tickets down at Opryland.
And Brenda and Sammy and Sharon and Sandy, Loretta and
  Buffy and May,
And Terri and Lynne at the Holiday Inn and Joey and Zoe
  and Faye.

Then Sherry and Rita, Diane and Anita, Olivia, Emmy and
Jean,

And Donna and Kay down at Elliston Place—right there in
the Pinto Beans.

Then Hazel and Carla and an ex-wife of Harlan's, then
Melva and Marge and Marie,

And three fat gospel singers who all come together in
perfect three-part harmony.'

He is humpin' the Queen of country music, when he hears
the Devil moan.

"Make it sweet, Billy Markham, but make it short, you've
got just thirty seconds to go.

And all of us here, we're applauding your show, and we'd
say you done right well,

And we just can't wait to hear you moan, when you're
fuckless forever in hell."

"Hold on!" says Billy, with one last thrust. "If I got thirty
seconds mo',

Then I got the right to one last hump before it's time to
go."

"Well, raise your voice and make your choice but you'd
better be quick and strong,

And make it a cum to remember, Bill—it's gotta last you
eternity long.

So who will it, who will it, who will it be? Who's gonna
be the one?

Starlet or harlot or housewife or hippie or grandma or
schoolgirl or black-robed nun?

Or fresh-scented Virgin or dope-smokin' groupie or sweet
ever-smilin' Stew?"

And Billy Markham, he stops ... and he looks at them all
and he says to the Devil ... "I think I'll ... take *you!*."

"Foul!" cries the Devil. "Foul, no fair! The rules don't hold
for me."

"You said man or woman or beast," says Billy, "and I
    guess you're all of the three."
And a roar goes up from the demons of Hell and it shakes
    the Earth across,
And the imps all squeal and the fiends all scream,
"He's Gonna Fuck the Boss!"
"Why you filthy scum." the Devil snarls, blushing a fiery
    red.
"I give you a chance to live again and you bust me in front
    of my friends."
"Hey, Play or Pay," Billy Markham says, "so set me free
    at last,
Or raise your tail and hear all hell, wail when I bugger your
    devilish ass."
"OK OK OK you win. Go on back to your precious Earth.
And plod along and plug your songs, but carry this lifelong
    curse.
You shall lust for a million women and not one's gonna
    come your way,
And you shall write ten million songs and not one's ever
    gonna get played.
And your momma and daughter and your own true love
    they gonna stay down here with me,
And you'll carry the guilt like a moveable Hell wherever
    the Hell you be."
So back on the streets goes Billy again, eatin' them
    Linebaugh's beans,
Singin' his songs while nobody listens and tellin' his story
    that no one believes.
And gets no women and he gets no hits but he says just
    what he thinks,
Hey, buy him a round ... it won't cost much ... ice water's
    all he drinks.
But try not to stare at the burns on his wrists as he wipes
    the sweat from his head,

As he tells how the Devil once burned him black
But he turned the Devil red.

BILLY, SCUZZY, AND GOD

We're at the Purple Peacock Rhinestone Bar, all the low are
    getting high,
And Billy tells his tale again to anyone who'll buy.
With waving arms and rolling eyes, he screams to the
    drunken throng,
"I've whipped the Devil and lived through Hell, now who's
    gonna sing my songs?"
Then from the shadows comes an oily voice. "Hey kid, I
    like your moves."
And out of the back limps a little wizened cat,
With black-and-white perforated wing-tipped shoes.
"Sleezo's the name," the little man says, "but I'm Scuzzy
    to my friends.
And I think I got a little business proposition you just
    might be interested in."
"Scuzzy Sleezo hisself," Billy Markham says. "Man,
    you're a legend in these woods,
You never cut the Devil down, but you done damn near as
    good.
Why, since I been old enough to jack, I been hearin' your
    greasy name,
It's an honor to meet an all-star, Scuzz. Where you setting
    up your game?"
"No more games for me," says Scuzzy, "I'm too old and
    too slow for the pace,
So I'm the world's greatest hustler's *agent* now and, Billy, I
    been studying your case.
I seen your first match with the Devil, and son, it was a
    Volkswagon/Mack truck collision.

And your second shot, well, you showed me a lot, but you
    got burned by a hometown decision.
And I says to myself, 'He can go all the way, with the
    proper guidance, of course.
The kid's got the heart, and with a few more smarts, he'd be
    an irresistable force.
Yeah, I can teach you the tricks and show you the shticks
    just like a hustler's training camp.
And I'll bring you on slow—then a prelim or so—then—
    Powee!—a shot at the Champ.'"
"The Champ?" says Billy Markham. "Now who in God's
    name is that?"
"Why God himself, says Scuzzy, you know anybody more
    champ than that?"
"Hey, a match with God?" Billy Markham grins.
"And what would be the purse?"
"Why a seat in heaven forever, of course, 'stead of livin'
    this no pussy, no hits, no nuthin' Nashville curse.
But I'll drive you like a wagon, son, and I'll sweat you like
    a Turk.
All for just fifty percent of the take—now sign here and
    let's get to work."

Now we find ourselves at the funky pool hall know as the
    Crystal Cue,
And the time is three months later, and the smoke is thick
    and blue.
And the pool table cloth is stained with tears and blood and
    ketchup spots.
As a fat old man with a dirty white beard stands practicin'
    three cushion shots.
"What are we doin' here?", says Billy to Scuzzy. "I been
    taught and I been trained.
And I don't need no more prelims, I am primed for the Big
    Big Game."

"Well son," says the old man, sinkin' the four, "why don't you pick yourself out a cue?"

"Hey, Santa Claus," Billy Markham snaps back, "wasn't nobody talkin' to you."

"Whoa, whoa," Scuzzy says, pullin' Billy aside ... "if you look close, you will notice his cue is a lightning rod.

And he ain't no Santa, and he ain't Fat Daddy ... you just insulted God."

"Well, hey, excuse me, Lord," says Bill, "I didn't mean to be uncool,

But it sure can shake a fellah's faith to find God hustling pool."

"Well where you expect to find me," says God, "on a throne with cherubs around?

Hey, I do that six days and nights a week, but on the seventh day ... I get down.

Besides I can't believe you came in here just to bat the breeze around."

"You're right about that, Lord," Billy says, "I come to take your crown."

"Beg pardon, Lord," says Scuzzy Sleezo, "I don't mean no disrespect.

But when you're dealing with my boy here, don't speak to him direct.

I'm his agent and representative and this kid is hotter than hot,

In his last match, he whipped the Devil, and now we're lookin' for a title shot."

"Beat the Devil, you say?" laughs God. "Well, I take my hat off to him.

Let him hang up his mouth and pick out a cue and he'll get the shot that's due him.

Any game he names—any table he's able--

Any price he can afford."

"Straight pool for heaven" says Billy Markham.

"Straight pool it is," says the Lord.

Crack—Billy Markham wins the break and bust 'em cool and clean.

The five ball falls, he sinks the seven, and then devastates the thirteen.

He makes the nine, and he bags the eleven, and he puts the six away, Then the three and the eight on a triple combination and he wins the game on a smooth masse.

He wins the next game, the next, and the next, and when he finally does miss,

He blows the dust off his hands, and his game score stands at 1376.

"Well, my turn at last," says the Lord chalkin' up,

"Son, you sure shoot a wicked stick.

I'll need some luck to beat a run like that: that is without resorting to miracles or tricks."

"Hey, trick and be damned." Billy Markham laughs.

"Tonight I'm as hot as flame.

So I laugh at your tricks—and I sneer at your stick— ...

And I take your *name* in *vain*."

"Oooh," goes the crowd that's been gathering around.

"Oooh," goes the rack boy in wonder.

"Oooh," says Scuzzy Sleezo, "I think you just made a slight tactical blunder."

"Oooh," says God, "you shouldn't have said that, son, you shouldn't have said that at all!"

And his cue cracks out like a thunderbolt spittin' a flamin' ball.

It sinks everything on the table, then it zooms up off the green.

Through the dirty window with a crash of glass and into the wind like a woman's scream,

Out of the pool hall, up through the skies,

The cue ball flames and swirls,

Bustin' in and out of every pool game in the world.

It strikes on every table, it crashes every rack.
And every pool ball in creation comes rebounding back!
Back through the window, they tumble and crash,
Down through the ceiling they spin.
A million balls rain down on the table, and every one goes
    in.
"Now, there," says Scuzzy Sleezo, "is a shot you don't see
    every day.
Lord, you should have an agent to handle your press, and
    build up the class of your play.
My partnership with this dirtbag here has come to a
    termination.
But God and Scuzzy Sleezo? Hey, that would be a
    combination."
Meanwhile, the cue ball flyin' back last, like a sputterin'
    fizzlin' rocket.
Goes weaving dizzily down the table
And—plunk! Falls right in the pocket.
"Scratch, you lose," yells Billy. "I thought you said you
    could shoot!"
"Scratch," says Scuzzy Sleezo. "I told you my boy'd come
    through."
"Scratch!" murmurs the crowd of hangers and hustlers.
"At last we have seen it all."
"Scratch!" mutters the Lord. "I guess I put a little too
    much English on the ball.
Just another imperfection, I never get it quite on the
    button.
Tell you what, son, I'll spot you three million balls and
    play you one more double or nothin'."
"Double what?" says Billy Markham. "I already whipped
    you like a child.
And I won my seat in heaven, now I'm gonna set it
    awhile."

"Hit-and-run chickenshit," sneers God. "You said you was the best.

Turns out you're just a get-lucky-play-it-safe pussy like all the rest."

"Whoa-whoa," says Billy. "There's somethin' in that voice I know quite well."

And he reaches out and yanks off God's white beard—and there stands the Devil himself!

"You said you was God," Billy Markham cries. "You conned me and hustled me, too!"

"I am God—sometimes—and sometimes I'm the Devil, good and bad, just like you.

I'm everything and everyone in perfect combination.

And everyone but you knows that there ain't no separation.

(*Sings*.) I'm everything and everyone in perfect combination. And everyone but you knows ...

"Please, please" says Billy Markham. "You ain't that great a singer,

And I would like to get to heaven before they stop serving dinner."

"Ok," says God, scribblin' somethin' down.

"Give this note to the angel on the wall.

And you sit up there and plunk your harp ...

Hey anybody wanna shoot some eight ball?"

So Billy walks out into the parkin' lot with stardust in his eyes,

(*Sings*.) "I got a seat in Heaven."

And he sees a golden staircase stretchin' up to paradise.

(*Sings*.) "I got a seat in Heaven."

And he grips the glittering balustrade, and begins his grand ascent.

(*Sings*.) "I got a ... "

"Just a minute, good buddy," yells Scuzzy Sleezo. "How about my fifty percent?

I helped you win the championship—and you wouldn't do
   ole Scuzzy Wuzzy wrong,
And since the purse is a seat in heaven, why, you just
   gotta take me along."
"Just a minute," says Billy Markham. "There's something
   weird going on in this game.
All the voices that I'm hearin' start to sound just the
   same."
And he rips off Scuzzy Sleezo's face and the Devil's
   standing there.
"Good God," yells Billy Markham, "are you—are you
   everywhere?"
"Yes I am," the Devil says. "And don't look so damn
   surprised.
I thought you could smuggle me into heaven wearing my
   Sleezy disguise.
'Course I could've walked in as Jehovah, but it just
   wouldn't have been the same.
But you and your corny Dick Tracy bit—you had to go and
   ruin my fantasy game.
Go on, climb your golden staircase, enjoy your paradise.
But don't rip off your own face, Bill—or you might get a
   shockin' surprise.
But, I'll be damned if I let you get to heaven climbin' that
   golden stairway."
And he plucks out Billy's soul and tees it up, and *whack*—
   drives it up the fairway.
And Billy floats out on a sea of light—on a snow white
   cloud he sails,
While vestal virgins comb his hair, and cherubs manicure
   his nails.
And up, up, to glory, Billy Markham sails away
And high high above him,
He hears his own songs being played

While down down below hear Scuzzy Sleezo curse his
    name,
To the click-click-click of the pool balls, As God hustles
    another game.

BILLY MARKHAM'S DESCENT

Billy Markham sits on an unwashed cloud, his hair is
    matted and mussed.
His dusty wings hang limp and grey and his harp strings
    have gone to rust.
With tremblin' hands and tear-stained cheeks, and a glazed
    look in his eyes,
He chews his nails and grinds his teeth, and stares across
    the skies.
But his thoughts are down in that nether world, in that
    burning fiery rain.
His thoughts are with his momma, how he longs to soothe
    her pain.
His thoughts are with his baby girl, how he'd love to ease
    her cryin'.
His thoughts are with his own true love, how he'd love to
    bust her spine
So late that night, while the heavenly harps play "In The
    Sweet Bye and Bye,"
Billy reaches for the silken rope that hangs down from the
    sky.
He has stripped himself of his crownand robes
He has clutched the silken cord:
As he swings himself down without a sound, so's not to
    wake the Lord.
Down he winds through the perfumed air, down through
    the marshmallow clouds.

And he hangs for a while o'er the city roofs,
Lookin' down at the scurryin' crowds.
Then down, down, through a manhole, to a stench he
    knows quite well.
Through the sewers of the street, till he feels his feet touch
    the shitmucked shores of Hell.
Then he scales the crusted rusted gates, he throws a bone to
    Cerebus Hounds.
And he swims the putrid river Styx, still down and further
    down.
Down past the gluttons, the dealers and pimps, down past
    the murderers' cage.
Down past the rock stars searching in vain for their names
    on the Rollin' Stone page.
Down past the door of The Merchants of War, past the
    puritans slop-filled bin
Past the Bigot's hive, till at last he arrives, at the pit
    marked BLAMELESS SINS.
And he finds the vat where his momma boils: and he raises
    her gently from the deep.
And he finds the grate where his little girl burns: and he
    lifts her and soothes her and rocks her to sleep.
And he finds the pit where his sweetheart sleeps: and he
    spits on the fire where she lay.
And he curses her as a whore of hell:
Curses and turns away,
"From this day on, I place my faith only in mother and
    child.
And never again shall I seek sweet salvation
In some bitch's scum stained smile.
Then back through the river he swims with them
Back over the gate he climbs,
And over the white hot coals he leaps, with the Hellhounds
    barking close behind.

Then back up the silken rope he climbs, up through the
    suffering swarms.
Past the clutching hands and the pitiful screams with his
    two precious loves in his arms.
Just one more pull, just one more pull—then free forever
    from Hell.
Just one more pull then—"Hello Billy!"—and there stands
    the Devil himself.
Only now he's wears his crimson robes and his horns are
    buffered bright.
And blood oozes through his white-linen gloves and his
    skin glows red in the night.
And his tail coils like an oily snake and the hell fires blaze
    in his eyes.
On those craggy rocks, he stands and blocks the way to
    paradise.
"Well, my, my, my, what have we here in my domain of
    sin?
In all my years as Prince of the Dark, this is the first case
    of anybody breaking in.
And all of the daredevil darin' dudes, well, who should the
    hero be?
But my old friend Billy Markham—who once made a punk
    out of me.
I heard you was in heaven, Billy, humpin' angels all day
    long,
What's a matter—did God get sick to his stomach listening
    to your raunchy songs?
You made me the laughing stock of hell, and the whole
    world laughed along with you.
Now here you come crashin' my party again:
Now tell me, just who's devilin' who?
Now, I didn't invite you down here, Bill, and nobody
    twisted your arm.

But you're back down here on my turf now, down here
    where it's cozy and warm.
So no more dice and no more games and no more jive
    stories to tell.
Just a the Devil and a man with three souls in his hand
    dangling between Heaven and ...
"But, hey what's this? Only *two*? Only *two* souls you've
    set free?
You must have forgot and left one behind: now who could
    that third one be?
Could it be your own true love, the one with the sweet wet
    smile?
The one you curse with each bitter breath 'cause she played
    with the Devil awhile?
You call yourself free? Tee hee tee hee. Why you prudish
    judgemental schmuck.
You'd leave your sweet love burn in hell for one harmless
    little suck.
What would you rather she had done, leaped in the boiling
    manure ...
So's you could keep your fantasy of someone sweet and
    pure?
She's a woman, flesh and blood and bone, and they do what
    they do what they do.
And right or wrong, she needs no curse from a hypocrite
    like you.
So, she shall rule with me—Billy Markham's love shall
    rule with me. She shall sit next to me on my throne.
And the whole world shall know—that the Devil's heart
    has more tenderness than your own.
So get your ass back up that rope, climb back to your
    promised land.
And hold your illusions of momma and daughter tight in
    your sweatin' hand.

But you'll see, you'll see, they're as human as she and
    you'll scream when you find it's true.
But please—stay up there and scream to God—Hell's gates
    are closed to you."
And Billy Markham, clutching his loves, climbs upward
    toward the skies.
And is it the sharp night wind that brings the tears to
    Billy's eyes?
Or is it the swirling sulphur smoke or the bright glare of
    the sun?
Or is it the sound of the wedding feast that the demons
    below have begun?

BILLY MARKHAM'S WEDDING

The trumpets of Hell have sounded the word like a
    screeching clarion call.
The trumpets of Hell have sounded the word and the word
    has been heard by all.
The trumpets of Hell have sounded the word and it reaches
    the heavenly skies.
Come angels, come demons, come dancing dead, the Devil
    is taking a bride.
And out of the Pearly Gates they come in a file two by
    two.
For when the devil takes a bride, there's none that dare
    refuse.
And Jesus himself, he leads the way down through the
    starless night.
With the Mother Mary at his left side and Joseph on his
    right.
And then comes Adam and then comes Eve and the saints
    move close behind.

And all the gentle and all the good, in an endless column
they wind.

Down, down to the pits of Hell, down from the heavens
they sift —Like fallen stars to a blood red sea, each
bearing the Devil a gift.

The strong and the brave, the halt and the lame, the deaf
and the blind and the dumb.

And last of all comes Billy Markham, cursing the night as
he comes.

Hell's halls are decked with ribbons of red and the feast has
been prepared.

And the Devil and his bride sit side by side in skull-and-
crossbone chairs.

And the Devil grins as his guests file in, for he is master
now.

And one-by-one they enter his realm—and one-by-one they
bow.

And the Devil whispers "Thank you, Friends," and he
swells his chest with pride.

"Come give me your blessings and place your gifts at the
feet of my blushing bride.

Lucrezia Borgia has made the punch of strychnine, wine
and gin.

And Judas has set the supper table on hallowed, bloody
linen.

The Feast is a human bar-b-cue, and the sauce is berri berri,

Chopped up by Lizzie Borden and cooked by Typhoid
Mary.

Here's some half-eaten apples fresh from the Garden of
Eden, (*Offers bucket.*)

Here's some tidbits from the Donner Pass.

Here's some fine old wine an acquaintance of mine

Made out of water, lemme fill your glass.

So you and you, drink of this crimson brew, we're all
brothers and sisters under the skin.

And take off your costumes of virtue and sin, and
Let the revels begin."
And slowly and shyly they strip off their wings, and hide
    their halos away.
And they shyly touch hands—and begin to dance, as hell's
    band begins to play.
There is Nero madly fiddlin' his fiddle, and Gabriel blowin'
    his horn.
And Idi Amin is beatin' his drum and Caligula's bangin'
    his gong.
Francis Scott Key plays piano and he is there cause he
    wrote that song.
And the pipes of Pan lead the Devil's band and everybody
    rocks along.
There's Janis and Elvis and Jimi and Cass, singin' them
    gimmesome blues.
And Adolph Hitler and Joan of Arc start doin' the
    boogaloo.
Lady Godiva jumps off her horse, and Kate Smith starts
    shakin' her hips.
And the Marquis de Sade does a promenade, laughin' and
    crackin' his whips.
Ghengis Khan got a tutu on, and he's doing a pirouette,
When out of the cake with a wiggle and a shake comes a
    naked Marie Antoinette.
And King Farouk he moons the crowd, while swingin'
    from the ceiling,
As Adam and the snake have one more drink just to show
    there's no hard feelings.
Isadora Duncan's gettin' kind of drunk and,
Doin' something filthy with her scarf,
And they bring out the turkey, and Jack the Ripper says
"Hey, I'll be glad to carve."
And there's old Dante dealing three card monte, Harpo Marx
    is tellin' jokes,

While Fatty Arbuckle is trying to collect the deposit on a
   bottle of Coke.
Elliot Ness shows up in a dress and Dillinger asks him to
   dance,
While Ivan the Terrible's tryin' to get into Susan B.
   Anthony's pants.
'N bare-ass naked on the balustrade sits Edgar Allen Poe,
Posin' for a two dollar caricature by Michelangelo.
Abraham Lincoln and John Wilkes Booth they're posin' for
   publicity photos,
While out in the foyer Richard the Third is comparing his
   hump with Quasimodo's.
And Catherine the Great, she's makin' a date with the horse
   of Paul Revere,
While Don Juan whispers love and lust into Helen Keller's
   ear.
And General MacArthur and Tokyo Rose, they're gigglin'
   behind the door,
While the daughters of Lot are yellin' "Hey, Pop, let's do it
   just once more."
And then John Wayne and Mary Magdelene announce
   they're going steady,
While Abel and Cain form a Daisy chain with Jeannette
   McDonald and Nelson Eddy.
And Doctor Faust and Johann Strauss, Nabokov and Errol
   Flynn,
They're arguin' over some teenaged girl that they're all
   interested in.
Lee Harvey Oswald's tryin' to make a phone call, getting in
   some target practice,
And Salome's in the hall playin' volleyball with the head
   of John the Baptist.
And Al Capone gives Eva Braun a big bouquet of roses,
And Gertrude Stein has a little more wine and hits on
   Grandma Moses.

Delilah she's clippin' and snippin' the snakes out of old
    Medusa's hair,
While Oscar Wilde says to Billy the Kid, "Can I show you,
    'round upstairs?"
And the Devil he sips his Boilin' Blood
And glances side to side
From the eyes of Billy Markham
To the eyes of his own sweet Bride
Then the music stops—and all heads turn—and the revelers
    freeze where they stand.
As Billy Markham approaches the throne and says, "May I
    have this dance?"
"And who be this?" the Devil snorts, "with the balls to
    think he can
Just walk up to the Devil's throne and ask the Devil's
    Bride to dance?
"Can this ... can this be Billy Markham, who loves only
    the chaste and the pure?
No, Billy wouldn't bow and kiss the hand of a woman he
    once called whore.
But whoever this poor, lonely wretch may be, it is my
    wedding whim.
That no man be refused this day—step down, darlin', and
    dance with him."
The Devil grins and waves his tail, the music begins again
    gentle and warm,
As the lady nervously steps from her throne into Billy
    Markham's arms.
And the guests all snicker and snigger and wait, And they
    watch the dancers' eyes,
As 'round and 'round the floor they swirl 'tween Hell and
    Paradise. (*Dances with mop.*)
"Oh, babydoll," says Billy Markham, "I've done you an
    awful wrong.

And to show you how rotten bad I feel, I even wrote about
    it in a song.
'I never should have called you a dirty whore, and I never
    should have spit on your bed.
And I never should of left you to burn here in Hell, 'cause
    you gave the Devil some head.
But if there's any hellish or heavenly way that I can make
    things right,
For your sweet sake, whatever it takes, I'll get you away
    tonight.'"
And the lady smiles a mysterious smile, as round the room
    they swing.
And she whispers low in Billy's ear; "Well, there is ... one
    little thing."

Now the hall is empty, the guests are gone, and there on
    the rusted throne,
Hand and hand in golden bands, the Devil and bride sit
    alone.
And the Devil stretches and yawns and grins, "Well, it's
    been quite a day,
And now it's time to seal our love in the usual mortal
    way."
And the Devil strips off his crimson cloak, and he casts his
    pitchfork aside,
And he frees his oily two-pronged tail, and waits to take
    his bride.
And his true love lifts her wedding dress up over her
    angel's head.
And hand in hand they make their way to the Devil's fiery
    bed.
And her upturned breasts glow warm in the fire, and her
    legs are shapely and slim.

And for the very first time since time began, the Devil
   feels passion in him.
"Now for the moment of truth," he whispers. "My love,
   my queen, my choice."
"I love you, too, motherfucker," she laughs—in Billy
   Markham's voice.
And the Devil leaps up and howls so loud that the fires of
   hell blow cold.
"Ain't no big deal," says Billy's voice. "While we was
   dancing, we swapped souls.
Now she's up in heaven singin' my songs and wearin' my
   body, too.
Safe forever in the arms of the Lord, while I'm down here
   in the arms of you."
"Why you creepin' crud" the Devil cries, "I'll teach you to
   fuck with my brain.
I'll give you a child who weighs ninety-five pounds, you
   wanna talk about screamin' pain!"
"Oh no, no no", says Billy Markham. "I will be your wife
   only in name—
You come near me with that double-pronged dick, and I'll
   rip it right off of your frame."
"Shhhh..." says the Devil. "Not so loud. If Hell learns
   what's been done.
They'll laugh me off this golden throne and damn me to
   kingdom come.
And you—You've given me my true love's body with a
   hustler's soul inside.
You know more of torture than I've ever dreamed—you're
   fit to be my bride."
"Well, don't take it so hard," Billy Markham says. "You
   know things could be worse.
Havin' *her* soul in *my* body—now, that would be a curse.
But you and me, we got lots in common, we both like to
   shoot the shit.

And we both like to joke, and we both like to smoke, and
    we both like to gamble a bit.
And that should be the makin's for a happy marriage, and
    since neither one of us is gonna die.
Well, we might as well start the honeymoon,––you wanna
    cut the cards or should I?"

Now the wedding night is a hundred years past and their
    garments have rotted to rags.
But face to face they sit in the flames, dealing five-card stud
    and one-eyed jacks.
And sometimes they play pinochle, sometimes they play
    gin.
And sometimes the Devil rakes in the pots, and sometimes
    the lady wins.
And sometimes they just sit and reminisce of the night
    they first were wed.
From dawn to dawn the game goes on ...
They *never* go to bed.

PROPERTY PLOT

The mop is a prop. It will become the Devil's walking stick, Red's guitar, Billy's cross in hell, the Demon's pitchfork, the Devil's golf club, Scuzzy's cane, God's pool cue, Bill's pool cue, the rope between heaven and hell, and the Devil's bride.

The bucket will become a slop bucket in hell, the Devil's throne, and a wedding feast serving bowl.

SKIN DEEP
Jon Lonoff

Comedy / 2m, 2f / Interior Unit Set

In *Skin Deep*, a large, lovable, lonely-heart, named Maureen Mulligan, gives romance one last shot on a blind-date with sweet awkward Joseph Spinelli; she's learned to pepper her speech with jokes to hide insecurities about her weight and appearance, while he's almost dangerously forthright, saying everything that comes to his mind. They both know they're perfect for each other, and in time they come to admit it.

They were set up on the date by Maureen's sister Sheila and her husband Squire, who are having problems of their own: Sheila undergoes a non-stop series of cosmetic surgeries to hang onto the attractive and much-desired Squire, who may or may not have long ago held designs on Maureen, who introduced him to Sheila. With Maureen particularly vulnerable to both hurting and being hurt, the time is ripe for all these unspoken issues to bubble to the surface.

"Warm-hearted comedy ... the laughter was literally show-stopping. A winning play, with enough good-humored laughs and sentiment to keep you smiling from beginning to end."
- TalkinBroadway.com

"It's a little Paddy Chayefsky, a lot Neil Simon and a quick-witted, intelligent voyage into the not-so-tranquil seas of middle-aged love and dating. The dialogue is crackling and hilarious; the plot simple but well-turned; the characters endearing and quirky; and lurking beneath the merriment is so much heartache that you'll stand up and cheer when the unlikely couple makes it to the inevitable final clinch."
- NYTheatreWorld.Com

COCKEYED
William Missouri Downs

Comedy / 3m, 1f / Unit Set

Phil, an average nice guy, is madly in love with the beautiful Sophia. The only problem is that she's unaware of his existence. He tries to introduce himself but she looks right through him. When Phil discovers Sophia has a glass eye, he thinks that might be the problem, but soon realizes that she really can't see him. Perhaps he is caught in a philosophical hyperspace or dualistic reality or perhaps beautiful women are just unaware of nice guys. Armed only with a B.A. in philosophy, Phil sets out to prove his existence and win Sophia's heart. This fast moving farce is the winner of the HotCity Theatre's GreenHouse New Play Festival. The St. Louis Post-Dispatch called Cockeyed a clever romantic comedy, Talkin' Broadway called it "hilarious," while Playback Magazine said that it was "fresh and invigorating."

Winner!
of the HotCity Theatre GreenHouse New Play Festival

"Rocking with laughter...hilarious...polished and engaging work draws heavily on the age-old conventions of farce: improbable situations, exaggerated characters, amazing coincidences, absurd misunderstandings, people hiding in closets and barely missing each other as they run in and out of doors...full of comic momentum as Cockeyed hurtles toward its conclusion."
- Talkin' Broadway

THE OFFICE PLAYS
Two full length plays by Adam Bock

THE RECEPTIONIST
Comedy / 2m, 2f / Interior

At the start of a typical day in the Northeast Office, Beverly deals effortlessly with ringing phones and her colleague's romantic troubles. But the appearance of a charming rep from the Central Office disrupts the friendly routine. And as the true nature of the company's business becomes apparent, The Receptionist raises disquieting, provocative questions about the consequences of complicity with evil.

"...Mr. Bock's poisoned Post-it note of a play."
- New York Times

"Bock's intense initial focus on the routine goes to the heart of *The Receptionist's* pointed, painfully timely allegory... elliptical, provocative play..."
- Time Out New York

THE THUGS
Comedy / 2m, 6f / Interior

The Obie Award winning dark comedy about work, thunder and the mysterious things that are happening on the 9th floor of a big law firm. When a group of temps try to discover the secrets that lurk in the hidden crevices of their workplace, they realize they would rather believe in gossip and rumors than face dangerous realities.

"Bock starts you off giggling, but leaves you with a chill."
- Time Out New York

"... a delightfully paranoid little nightmare that is both more chillingly realistic and pointedly absurd than anything John Grisham ever dreamed up."
- New York Times

SAMUELFRENCH.COM

CPSIA information can be obtained at www.ICGtesting.com
Printed in the USA
BVOW020059090112

280085BV00004B/1/P